Letters *to a*
Young Seeker

Letters *to a* Young Seeker

Departing Thoughts from an Elder

Neale Donald Walsch
with poetry by Em Claire

Books may be purchased through booksellers or by contacting Sacred Stories Publishing.

Letters to a Young Seeker: Departing Thoughts from an Elder
Neale Donald Walsch
with poetry by Em Claire

Tradepaper Print ISBN: 978-1-958921-81-4
Electronic Book ISBN: 978-1-958921-82-1
Library of Congress Control Number: 2025950385

Published by Sacred Stories Publishing
Printed in the United States of America

Table of Contents

My Heart is with You

It's not easy, this trip that each of us are on.

And my heart is with you, as you encounter this age-old journey--yet one that will be individual to you...

I've been on the journey for 82 years, and I will offer here my humble sharing of what someone who's been around that long has encountered and concluded. I hope that this can be of some value to you, and I can tell you that I sure wish someone had said to me, when I was in my 20s, even a little of what I'm going to share with you here.

Or, gosh, even when I was in my 30's.

The truth is, I would have been happy to have had these ideas to consider even in my 40's.

So now, my dear soul friend, I will share what these letters to you will look like.

I'm going to make 21 statements, each one of which will be the focal point of a separate short letter I've written to you. Every letter will then be followed by a gentle reflection from the published works of the American poet Em Claire, my beloved wife and life partner, who has shown me that poetry can often open the heart in a way which allows the mind to embrace the more mystical side of life, rather than filtering life through an always logical lens. This, of course, is what the Arts have always done for humanity.

Having said this, I wish to now take note of the German poet Rainer Maria Rilke, who produced a series of messages from 1903 to 1908 to a young, would-be poet on how to survive as a sensitive observer in a harsh world. After Rilke's passing, the recipient of his messages published them as a short volume, entitled *Letters to a Young Poet*. The idea for this book, and its title, are clearly an homage, and although nothing of Rilke's letters are referenced or re-produced here, we hope that what we have offered on these pages will also be a handhold, a bread crumb on the trail, a stone on the path as you walk into your own sacred remembering.

I have chosen to refer to each of the 21 statements highlighting my letters as an Inner Awareness, because it is my understanding that Earth is not a school in which we are invited to learn what there is to know about life. While some people have said that this is precisely what our time on Earth is about, I am proposing here that it is about bringing *forward* the wisdom that *already exists* within each of us.

I know that you are now choosing to do precisely that, or you would never have begun reading a book such as this...

I left Home so long ago now
that I would not recognize my own face.

I constructed the Boat of my Life
and I set out
into the open sea,
waving to all who knew
that the seas would give me
everything I could handle,
and everything I could not—

and yet they waved, and I set out
into the open sea
in the Boat of My Life:

built from Soul, crafted by Heart.
And with great innocence I pushed off

into the open sea

and have been away from my Home
so long now that I would not recognize my own face—

but I know that Home

Home
remembers me.

For the First Time

Dear Young Seeker...

Hello, my friend. I don't know how old you are, but I assume you're many decades younger than me. I'm clear that what the world needs in this moment are more human beings such as you, with your kind of willingness to be not only open-minded, but open-hearted—and, if I could coin a phrase, open-souled.

(By that I mean, open to the wisdom within.)

Now please don't let what I've just said stop you short. My use of the word "soul" does not mean that what I'm going to offer you in these letters is an ongoing religious tract, or a spiritual discourse. It's not even necessary to believe that a being such as "God" exists for you to reap benefit from the comments about how life works that I'll be sending you here.

You may wish to read these letters one per day, one per week, one per month, or all at once. Pick the pace that works for you and feels natural in your flow.

To get you started, let me summarize in nine words the overall message that I've come here to share with you after my eight decades on life's journey. This may just be life's biggest secret.

Here is...

Inner Awareness #1

There's more going on here than meets the eye.

Sincerely,

Neale

You never really know
when it will come.

Rising, laying foot
into the same imprint
you've made
yesterday
and the day before
and yes,
eternally before.

But some time
that superbly hairline crack
in your well-preserved casing
will suffer *a Grace*.

You can call it crisis, or crumble,
or, you can see it
as the first time your Truth
has succeeded in escaping,

like the soft and persistent
pressings of a chick

ready to leave the egg,

ready to *know* Life

for the first time.

Beautiful Dreamer

Dear Young Seeker...

*H*ave you ever had a dream which seemed to reveal something to you that was very important, yet you didn't fully understand it?

I had such a dream when I was very young. I want to say I was about 9 or 10.

In the dream, I was moving through what felt like home movies of my just-getting-started life. You know, scrambling out of bed and going to school, fumbling with my physical ineptness at every outdoor game until the kids on the playground never wanted me on their team anymore, eating dinner with my family and watching my brother being praised up and down for whatever he said or did...that sort of thing.

My dream suddenly switched to images of my parents as I saw each of *them* moving through *their* life. My dad getting up and going to work every morning, my mom cleaning the house, occupying us with her attentions, preparing the dinner we were all going to eat that evening...and, distressingly, both of them arguing with each other a lot, with raised voices, pounded tables, slammed doors, and then The Cold Treatment. (Refusing to talk to each other for the rest of the day—and sometimes, for much of a weekend).

The emotional upheaval of the remembered arguments woke me out of my dream, and I remember feeling something very strange. That feeling was reduced in my mind to two words.

Nothing Matters.

This thought pulled me out of my sleep. *Nothing matters???*, I asked myself. How can that be? Surely it matters that Mom and Dad argue so much. Surely it matters that nobody at the playground wants me on their team anymore. Surely it matters that my brother gets all the praise, and that all it felt I was receiving was correction and criticism.

Sadly, it wasn't until I was much, much older that I came to...

Inner Awareness #2

Nothing has any meaning,
save the meaning you give it.

When I said "much, much older," I wasn't exaggerating. I was entering my 50th year on this planet before I reached this realization. Before then, I thought that if I lost my job, it meant something. I also thought that if my boss praised my work, it meant something. I thought that if I lost an argument, it meant something. I also thought that if I won an argument, it meant something. I thought that if I disobeyed one or more of God's commands (I was told about those when I was 9), it meant something. I also thought that if I obeyed God's commands, it meant something.

Then—all at once, very much as in my childhood dream—Inner Awareness #2 arrived in my consciousness. I saw that nothing mattered intrinsically, or inherently. That is, in and of itself. We *give* every event in life *the meaning* that it has for us.

I'd like to tell you how and why this became apparent to me, because it could change your own life for the better, much earlier than your late 40s or your 50s.

So, if you feel that it might serve you, move on to my next letter.

Sincerely,

Neale

Beautiful Dreamer
Who Are You,
sitting in the seat of this soul?
Bless your innocent eyes,
half closed.
Bless your tender jaw,
still set in confusion.
Bless your full, beating heart,
so kissed with Light.

Bless the hand that writes,
and the breath that hesitates,
and the World that waits

for You.

Know Yourself as Light

Dear Young Seeker...

There's one thing—a single perception, really—that brought me to my awareness that nothing has any meaning, save the meaning I give it. I began asking myself: What is the true nature of this "I" who is deciding what things mean, by coming up with significant interpretations of circumstances and events?

I hope you ask yourself that question long before I did, because if you are still in your 20s or your 30s, there is something you may greatly benefit from knowing about the "I" that is you.

I've labeled it...

Inner Awareness #3
You are not simply a physical entity,
you are a spiritual being.

When I was young, I saw myself as having a body and a mind. I didn't give serious thought to the idea that I had what is called a "soul". Oh, I heard talk about that, of course. I simply didn't pay much attention to what it could mean, as a practical matter on a day-to-day basis, to be more than a physical life form.

What about you? Do you have a particular thought about this?

If your current idea is that you are basically a physical entity seeking to get through your days and nights without being stymied by the seemingly endless challenges and continuing struggles of human existence, you will see life in a way which focuses much of your attention and most of your effort on finding solutions to the problems, and creating victory over the obstacles, which you experience yourself encountering.

If, on the other hand, you believe that you are a spiritual being, you will surely wonder more than once why a spiritual entity would find itself beset with one challenge after another. There must be a reason for life being the way it is, your mind will insist. At least, there had *better* be, or very little of this life will make much sense to you.

Well, my observation and my experience is that there is. I strongly encourage you to hold this thought in your daily awareness, because it creates an immensely empowering context within which to explore the *purpose* behind all of life—which we'll begin to do in my next letter.

Sincerely,

Neale

Know Your Self as Light.
Bigger even than Breath.
Larger even than the Whole.
Quieter even than the Quiet that holds You.

Know Your Self as Held.
Softer even than as before;
Deeper even than any Darkness.

When the Lightbody of You
breathes without borders--
knows not
even of the concept,
or of any bounds at all...

When you Know Your Self
as only Light,
summoning The Mystery
to move through you—
exquisite, innocent instrument
of the long
long, eternity of song—
then
Know Your Self as
Life's greatest Laughter,

Life's greatest Lover,
beckoning the Mystery

come hither.

We Are Lightbabies

Dear Young Seeker…

Let's look seriously at this idea: If you really are a spiritual entity and not simply an expression of life in a physical form, then what is the purpose of your being in a physical body?

And does realizing and accomplishing that purpose produce the experience of real happiness, meaningful achievement, and personal fulfillment on Earth?

My 82-year life has served to convince me of three things:

A: We all *are* spiritual beings. (Yes, I call each such being a "soul".)

B: There *is* a very special reason that we are living in a body with a mind.

C: Achieving our purpose in being in that body with a mind *does* lead to a life in which we experience downward turns with little emotional pain, and in which we make few, if any, of the kind of mistakes that cause others pain.

I have found an important key in all this to be...

Inner Awareness #4

The purpose of your life has little to do with what your mind may think, or your body may desire.

This is not bad news for your mind or your body however, because when you focus on your *soul's* reason for being in the physical world, the change in your life's focus, intention, and motivation can produce miracles in your Earthly adventure.

Not only the gift of no longer causing others pain, or the dissolving of emotional turmoil in your own life, but miracles of manifestation which can produce both the physical outcomes and the spiritual experiences of your dreams.

The ability to produce such miracles is a product of your evolution, which some people may think takes a long time. Yet in truth, it is happening as fast as the snap of a finger.

Let me put this another way. Evolution is ongoing in every moment. It is what is going on right now. It never stops. And while it may take longer to reach a particular level than some of us would like, there is never an instant when it is not occurring.

Once you understand this, only one question remains: How long will it take—and *what* will it take—for your own evolution to get to the point where you can find yourself released from the pain, the stress, and the strain of everyday life, and begin remembering, demonstrating, and expressing more of the joy in life for which you have been yearning?

I believe that for you, on this day as you are reading this, the answer to that question revolves around how seriously you consider, and how soon you embrace as part of your way of moving through the world, Inner Awareness #4. It is based on, and emerges from, Inner Awareness #3, which reminds you that you are not simply a physical entity, you are a spiritual being.

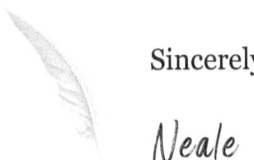

Sincerely,

Neale

We are Lightbabies.
Golden Grace.
Wings meant for flight.
We are delicate, and pregnant
with goodness.
We are each made of such a quiet
that the entire Universe
can hear us.

There is only the Opening, the Unfolding
ever happening.
All else are thoughts—
lollipops for the mind.

We are Lightbabies,

parading

as Humankind.

Show Yourself to Me

Dear Young Seeker...

I made a pretty strong statement in my last note, which I feel deserves further scrutiny. I said that "when you focus on your soul's reason for being in the physical world, the change in your life's focus, intention, and motivation can produce miracles in your Earthly adventure."

This statement is based, of course, on the premise that you embrace (if only as an intellectual excursion) Inner Awareness #3. To refresh your memory, that Awareness is that you are not simply a physical entity, you are a spiritual being.

Now, as you know from Inner Awareness #2, nothing has any meaning, save the meaning you give it. If you give significant meaning to the statement that you are more than merely a corporal life form, such as a bird in the sky or a fish in the sea, but have a spiritual identity as *well* as a physical one, you may no doubt find yourself asking at some point in your life: "Why would spiritual beings put themselves through this physical life, with all the problems and challenges it presents? What is the point of all this?"

Fair question.

My understanding is that our spiritual being—what I have called, as I said earlier in these letters, our "soul"—has something very specific that it seeks to accomplish with its passage through physical life. It has not been forced to come here. Such a thing would not be possible, given that every sentient being in the cosmos is endowed with free will.

So, what is the wish of the soul?

I have come to understand that it desires to experience what it knows itself to be. And I believe that what each soul knows itself to be is an individual expression of Life's Primal Energy. Or, if you believe in God, an Individuation of Divinity.

As well, I believe that the essence of the primal energy is always benevolent, in that its very function is to serve life itself, and that it cannot serve life if it works against life's purpose.

28

I have concluded, then, that everything which happens in life produces benefit—even if, and when, it does not appear to—because each event and circumstance provides an opportunity for the soul to demonstrate, express, and experience its true identity as an Individuation of Divinity.

This has brought me to...

Inner Awareness #5

*You have come to the physical realm
to serve your soul's agenda.*

If we are truly spiritual beings, why not stay in the spiritual realm and serve our agenda there? Another good question. And the answer is that the soul enters the physical realm because this realm is a contextual field which contains that which is "other than" who we are.

We can know, demonstrate, express, and experience who we are only in the space of who we are not. And *that* is why spiritual beings put themselves through this physical life, with the challenges it presents.

I'm going to trust that you have a determination to know more about this, because I sense that *you* sense that Inner Awareness #1 offers an insight that really and truly *could* change your life for the better. Namely: There *is* "more going on here than meets the eye."

Sincerely,

Neale

"Show yourself to me," said I to God again.
And this is what happened next:

I became pregnant with Light.
My eyes were sunrise and sunset, both.
Freckles announced themselves planets and stars,
and beamed upon my cheeks.
Each of my lips became a kiss to the other,
my ears heard oceans of life.
Between my eyes there was an indigo wheel,
between my toes, blond fields.
My hands remembered climbing trees,
my hair, each lover's fingers.

And then I whispered,
"But why have you made me this *way?"*
And it was told to me this:
"Because I have never had Your name before,
nor heard the way You sing it.
Nor stared into the universe through eyes like These.
Nor laughed This way, nor felt the path that
These tears take.

Because I have not known These ecstasies,
nor risen to These heights, nor experienced

every nuance of the innocence
with which You create Your lows.

Nor how a Heart could grow so wide,
or break so easily,
or Love

quite *so unreasonably*."

Nothing Needs Fixing

Dear Young Seeker,

I am going to introduce you now to the Law of Opposites. That is, if you have not already heard of it.

There are, as we all know, several "laws of life" which we have been told about, at least in general terms, in our upbringing. There's the Law of Gravity—which, of course, we've all experienced—and other laws, such as the Law of Thermodynamics, Newton's Law of Motion, the Law of Quantum Mechanics, etc., all of which we can learn about if we take certain courses in our schools and colleges. But nowhere (unfortunately) have I seen a course in the Law of Opposites.

The Law of Opposites says this: "In the absence of that which you are not, that which you are, is not. "

That is, it is not experienceable.

Because you came to the physical realm to demonstrate, express, and thus experience who you really are as an individuation of life's Essential Essence, you definitely need to know about this axiom.

Here's an example of how it works: If you are six feet tall, and everything else in the world is also exactly six feet tall—every tree, every blade of grass, every building, every hill, every person—you will never be able to experience being six feet tall. You could *know* that you are six feet tall, but you would have no idea what it is *like* to *be* six feet tall.

Similarly, you can have no experience of what you call "fast" without what you call "slow," no experience of what you call "here" without what you call "there," no experience of what you call "up" without what you call "down." And, using more impactful examples, there is no experience of what you call "good" without what you call "evil," or what you call "happiness" without what you call "sadness," or what you call "success" without what you call "failure," and so on.

None of this was ever explained to me when I was young. Not even, for that matter, when I was in my 30s or 40s. It wasn't until my fifth decade on the planet that I came to understand why virtually every spiritual master in Earth's history has offered us what is essentially the same message, each in their own words and in their own way.

My own summary and personal version of this message follows: Raise not your fist to heaven and curse the darkness not. Rather, be a light *unto* the darkness, that you might know who you really are... and that all those whose life you touch might know who they really are as well.

So that you don't have to wait until your own 50s, I offer this...

Inner Awareness #6

The moment you declare yourself to be anything
(successful, abundant, happy, etc.),
its exact opposite will appear
in your awareness.

When you see this as a gift, not an obstacle, you will have discovered how to use the Law of Opposites the way you've discovered how to use the Law of Gravity. The Laws of Life are designed to help you *get* your way, not to get *in* your way.

So, when the opposite of what you have declared and desire appears in your awareness, let yourself greet it with a knowing smile and an open mind, rather than frustration, agitation, or anger.

To offer an example: If what you have declared and desire is greater financial stability, and the very next day a completely forgotten large bill unexpectedly arrives in the mail, or something breaks down in your car that you know is not going to be inexpensive to repair, allow yourself to confidently know that this seemingly opposing energy is simply arising as a powerful opportunity for you to know and be clear that all will be taken care of in the long run.

Then, don't be at all surprised if you find yourself doing just fine—or even better than just fine—five weeks or five months later, and let yourself be aware that the Law of Opposites has done nothing more than arouse your determination to embrace the part of you that you chose to experience.

Sincerely,

Neale

God says for me to tell you this:
Nothing needs fixing;
everything desires
a
Celebration.

You were made to bend
so that you would find
all of the many miracles at your feet.
You were made to stretch
so that you could discover
your own beautiful face of Heaven
just above
all that you think you must shoulder.

When I appeal to God to speak to me,
I'm feeling just as small and alone as you might be.
But this is when, for no particular reason at all,
I begin to

shine.

Please Do Not Regret

Dear Young Seeker

The Law of Opposites definitely produces challenges in life. Yet my experience has been that once we look deeply into what is going on behind the simple appearance of things, our day-to-day life can change in a way that virtually eliminates its worst emotional aspects.

This is not to say there will be no sadness, but it is to say that we need not suffer from painful experiences. Which brings me to...

Inner Awareness #7
*Pain and suffering are
not the same thing.*

My life has shown me that physical or emotional pain is what I experience during or after a particular event or occurrence. Suffering, on the other hand, is what I experience along with the pain when I decide that what is happening should not be happening.

An example I like to use when I explain this is that of a woman in childbirth. She will surely experience pain, but she may not necessarily experience it as suffering. In fact, she may experience it as just the opposite, finding herself shedding tears of joy even as she feels the pain.

When I came to understand in my 50's that every moment of pain in the first five decades of my life was part of the birthing of a new "me"—or, if you please, a movement forward in my own evolution—my mental and emotional suffering from past painful events came to an end, even if both the memory of those events and any physical pain produced by those events remained present in my mind and my body.

As an author, I have had the opportunity to present many lectures through the years, and in almost every presentation I have made, I have asked my audience to answer, with a show of hands, this question: "How many of you have experienced, while it was happening, what you felt was one of the worst things that could happen to you,—only to realize two weeks, or two months, or two years later that it was one of the best things that ever happened to you?"

Nearly always, 95% of the audience raises a hand.

Why is this such a common experience? The reason is that people *evolve* as a result of even unwelcome events, and their expanded emotional, physical, psychological, and spiritual maturity brings them to a new level of awareness regarding how they have grown as a person because of what happened. They see the long-term benefit of what appeared at first to be a totally non-beneficial experience.

This is not a small thing. Evolution is, in fact, the implanted, embedded, and ingrained process and goal of all of life. It is the "more than meets the eye" that is going on in this physical realm.

My clarity around this is what has allowed me to hold all the occurrences of my life—past and present—in a new way; a way that has dramatically improved both my present experience and my future outlook. It can, likewise, dramatically alter yours, virtually eliminating suffering as you journey onward.

If you think it might serve you to hear more about removing suffering from your life, I invite you to read on.

Sincerely,

Neale

Please do not regret
all those moments that have brought you
Here.
If you are reading this,
then your perseverance has been answered,
and a Grace is coming.

So for now, hold on loosely to where you are.
And like knots on a rope that mark your reaching,
hand over hand
you will continue to climb:
sometimes through ecstasy,
sometimes through white agony,
but
higher
into ever more Light.

This same formula over and over again,
until that day you find yourself:

Just a beacon. Only flame.

In a place

where even Love Itself has come undone...

Is It Made of Love?

Dear Young Seeker,

I promised in my first letter that this series of personal missives would not be a religious tract or a spiritual discourse, and it will not. But we do need to simply touch very briefly on the subject of "God", because much of what our species has been told on the whole topic of good and evil, saints and sinners, heaven and hell, and what, if anything, happens after death, drives the engine of billions of human beings, producing day-to-day behaviors which impact all of us.

Having been encouraged by their religions to live in a godly fashion, many people imitate what they've been told about our deity, telling others what *they* require in order to be happy, then condemning and punishing those individuals or nations not doing as they demand. Many of those doing the demanding think nothing of this, because, after all, a way of behaving that's good enough for God should be good enough for us, no?

One result of this is that we have had armed conflict on this planet for all but 5% of recorded history.

Few people realize that there are over 4,200 religions now on Earth. This translates into something of noteworthy significance: billions upon billions of humans believe and obey what those faith traditions tell them.

And what do most of those denominations tell them? They say that the God whom they say exists is an all-powerful entity who loves us for sure, but who also issues demands regarding human behavior, then observes and judges our thoughts, words, and deeds, condemning and punishing us if we do not behave in the way we have been commanded to behave, as well as provide the fall-to-our-knees worship that many religions contend is required.

The fallout from this is that many members of our species believe that God's relationship with us is transactional. It is a *quid pro quo.* "You give me what I require, and I'll give you what you want."

Now what does all this have to do with you, as a young seeker? Well, it can help you understand why some people, or groups of people, act the way they do, and it can also offer you an invitation to change your own mind about God—if you think there is such thing as God at all.

I've come here to share with you my experience, so that you can avoid walking into some of the walls I crashed into headfirst in my own early years.

Here's one of the most important conclusions I've come to...

Inner Awareness #8
God may not be what
many people think God is.

While these letters are not intended to be a religious discourse or an espousal of theological doctrine, I think it important to notice that even people who don't believe in God at all have no doubt heard a bit (if not a great deal) from those who do. And so, it's clear to me that Inner Awareness #8 is worthy of at least cursory consideration.

Maybe we should change the single word that is used to refer to the Higher Power in our universe.

Maybe we should not call it "God", but rather, call it "Goodness."

Sincerely,

Neale

I don't know if my god is the same
as your god:

Is It made of Love?

Does it want for you what you want for you?
Does it come to you with hands open,
asking nothing, but ready for anything?

Does it whisper to you of
Light, and of Stillness,
and point you toward *any*
of the paths that will take you there?

Does it remind you of your Seeing?
Does it remind you of your Knowing?

Does it remind you of the gentlest Lover
ever you've dreamed,
caressing a weariness from your heart?

Is it ever late?
Is it ever gone?
Is it made of Love?

When Did You Stop Singing?

Dear Young Seeker,

There is an aspect of the physical realm which could be the most important part of our lives. Yet important as I have found it to be, it may be one of the facets of life that is least understood and used by many people.

Because it is not as widely understood as it could be, it is more widely ignored than it should be. I am talking about metaphysics. And I am writing you this letter so that you will not ignore it.

I'll begin by declaring that everything in existence is made up of energy. Now that may seem to be patently obvious, but what may not be so obvious is how energy *affects* energy.

Energy impacts upon itself. That is important enough to be worth repeating, so let me repeat it: *Energy impacts upon itself.*

Energy is life's foundational essence. All things—from physical phenomena such as wind and snow, light and temperature, to objects such as grass and trees, mountains and people, to words such as those you are reading here, or may speak to someone later, to feelings such as love and fear, anger and joy, and even thoughts such as whether this book is even mildly interesting are comprised of this foundational essence.

How everything in our world is created, and how it looks or sounds or feels, depends on how its energy is vibrating. That is, the rate of oscillation.

What is fascinating is that we can exert personal control over this oscillation in some of the things mentioned above—and this control can produce particular and specific outcomes in our physical environment.

It is because this is true that the next statement is also true.

Inner Awareness #9
You are the creator of
your own reality.

Life's key question is not whether you are creating your reality, but whether you are doing it intentionally or unintentionally, purposefully or accidentally.

What could be called "applied metaphysics" is the intentional, deliberate, calculated, and conscious use of thoughts, words, and feelings to create a particular effect or outcome in the physical world.

To put all this plainly and directly: positive thoughts, words, and feelings more often than not create positive circumstances, events, and outcomes in everyday life, because of the way in which they vibrate. The same is true of negative thoughts, words, and feelings. This is because the vibratory rate of energy tends to attract energy of a similar oscillation.

In a sense, this makes us *all* like gods, producing much of our daily reality, with our thoughts, words, and feelings acting as magnets. They are *attractors*. They pull toward the person who is the source, more of what is being sourced.

Now it's all very well and good to say, "Project only positive thoughts, words, and feelings." But what if your honest feelings about something are simply not positive?

Another fair question. We'll answer it in the next letter.

Sincerely,

Neale

This morning God asked me,
"When did you stop singing?"

At first, I was angered.
Then, I let the question be.

"Why," said I,
"I believe it was when I began to follow
every thought that was given to me
by my parents,
and then by my peers,
and then by any passing stranger.
I believe it was the moment I began to choose
achievement over Alchemy
and competition over Compassion.
It was that morning I rose,
and put my feet into shoes
too tight for Freedom;
when I listened, instead of Music,
to mankind."

"I believe," said I, "that I stopped singing
the moment I stopped hearing Birdsong
or laughed with the sounds of Laughter."

"And when did you stop dancing?" said God.
"Or being enchanted by stories?
Or stop finding comfort in the sweet territory
of silence?"

"Why," answered I, "It was, you see, when I forgot
that

I
am
You."

It Is Your Own Life That You Desire to Cherish

Dear Young Seeker,

Many people—if and when they find themselves in a negative frame of mind—might say, "I can't help it. *That's just how I feel!*"

Yet the fact is, feelings need not be only things that come over us. They can be things we overcome. That is, feelings can be chosen. They can be consciously selected. If we don't like a feeling which has come over us, we can overcome that feeling.

Some people have said, "I was overcome by emotion." Fair enough. That was their experience. But as already noted, emotion is energy-in-motion, and it is *we* who *put* it into motion by our decision about particular occurrences or circumstances, situations or experiences.

Being overcome by emotion is a response. And—to make the point indelible—for most people, emotional response proceeds from their thought. This could be either an idea held beforehand about how something should or should not be, or their first thought following an event or occurrence.

It may seem as if we can't *help* the way we feel in certain moments or situations, but we can. And one way to do this is to literally choose what we feel by choosing the feeling that we hold and project after—or even before— encountering or hearing about anything.

The mind is lightning fast in its response to outward events or experiences, but here is something that most people may not realize: Most present moment thoughts are based on prior thoughts about virtually everything that is occurring in life. Many of us hold ideas about how things should be, and our reactions to how things are occurring are based on those prior thoughts. But our responses can be intentional *creations*. They do not have to be unintentional *reactions*.

If you look at those two terms closely, you will see that "creation" and "reaction" are almost the same words. It's just that the "c" and the "r" reside in different places. I like to say that when you put the "c" first and the "r" second, then you can "C" who you really "R"! And who you are is—as we noted in Inner Awareness #7—the creator of your own reality.

I'm making this point for a reason. I'm going to suggest here that it's the *emotions* we create with our thoughts that are even more powerful tools than thoughts themselves. This is not something that is taught in most circles where "positive thinking" is espoused.

I believe much more attention could and should be directed to the emotions we choose. Indeed, I believe this is the first place we should look if we wish to create a peaceful, joyful, wonder-filled life. I observe that it's here where our most powerful creative force is born.

I therefore share with you this note as...

Inner Awareness #10
Your emotions are your life's most powerful creative tool.

There's a very meaningful difference, believe me, between thoughts and emotions. A person can have a thought and pay very little attention to it, or even completely ignore it, deciding it is not necessary or not welcome. But once a person translates an idea, which is a relatively benign energetic vibration, into an emotion, which is a much more energetically condensed vibration, they can find themselves opened to an energetic sensation which creates far more impact in a person's body. And if the emotion is felt strongly enough, its energy projects *through* that person and *from* that person into their exterior environment.

This accelerates the process of personal creation, producing outcomes more rapidly and more profoundly than one might realize.

What I am saying here is that when people become emotional over what they have been thinking, their energy reverberates most rapidly, most powerfully, and projects most widely. Choose carefully, then—choose *very* carefully—the emotions that you express most often as you move through life. And when you feel overcome by emotion, overcome any tendency to express an emotion that doesn't serve you in a positive way.

This doesn't mean to deny an honest emotion, but it does mean to use emotions intentionally. In other words, to feel a certain way on purpose. As a creation, not a reaction.

In my next letter I am going to suggest a daring—one might almost say a revolutionary—change in the emotions you choose to feel and to express. Hold onto your seat. This would be a major...truly *major*...shift.

Sincerely,

Neale

It is your own life that you desire to cherish
like one brings the downy tuft of a Dandelion to the
lips
blows softly
prays
to give everything away
keep
only what remains
of a life well lived
a life well loved
nourished and blessed
by the suns and by the soils
and by whatever it was
that
finally

opened you

What Is It That You Were Given?

Dear Young Seeker,

I hope you'll agree that what I've offered in this book has been practical, down-to-earth, boots-on-the-ground advice on how to get from where you are to where you want to be in this life.

That said, we've now come to a place within my own life's closing thoughts, where I'm going to explore a powerful tool that one can use to move more easily, more joyously, more painlessly, and more lovingly through life—and I'm going to make another passing mention of the Divine.

What I'm going to propose here uses what I see as the primal energy of life in such a powerful way that it could change your whole life for the better virtually overnight. What is great about it is that—as I made clear earlier—you don't have to believe in God or hold an idea of God in a particular way by adopting and embracing a particular religion, to use the tool. You only have to believe that the primal energy of life is what is best defined as pure love.

And it is.

If you've ever seen the look on a mother's face as she holds her newborn baby, you have seen pure love.

If you've ever witnessed the feelings flowing between a couple as they are being married, you have seen pure love.

If you've ever watched a man hug his child after watching that child protect a younger sibling from being seriously hurt, you have seen pure love.

So, most people are clear that pure love exists, and they know that it's the kind of love that needs, expects, requires and demands nothing in return. It is an energy that can help, heal, and hearten any moment.

And now, here is that daring, revolutionary idea of how you can use that energy as a tool: Make an important switch. *Replace* thought with emotion as the item in your metaphysical toolbox to which you'll now pay the most attention, and of which you'll make the most use.

But do not use the first emotion that comes up for you in any given situation, unless it is the way that you believe pure love would best be expressed.

This brings us to...

Inner Awareness #11

When you cause your emotion to always be an expression of pure love, you will change your life for the better forever.

The question is, can a normal person do this? And what about (as we mentioned earlier) when you don't truly feel pure love? Are you to abandon how you do feel, forsake your truth, and "fake it"?

My answer to the last inquiry is no. Even anger can be expressed lovingly. So too, frustration. And, as well, disappointment or disapproval. It turns out that any thought which one would define as negative can be expressed in a positive way.

Whoa...that was an important statement. Please don't let that one go in one ear and out the other. I'm going to suggest that you repeat that to yourself...and maybe even write it on your bathroom mirror with a felt-tip pen, so that you will see it every day. It may at first seem to defy all reason, but it is true.

Even the most negative thought can be expressed in a positive way.

More on that, and on how we can beneficially choose all of our emotions, in our next letter.

Sincerely,

Neale

What is it that you were given?
I mean from the loss.
After what was taken.
That very thing you could never live without.
The person or place;
the secret, or circumstance—
now that it is gone,
or has been found out,
and you can no longer call *it* foundation

what is it that you were given?

You know, and I know, this:
there is a hollowing out.
Something comes and opens you up

right
down
the
middle

and from that moment on
you are no longer immune to this world.

You wake, you wander,

every familiar, now a foreign.
You walk as through water
until you make it back to your bed,
and finally, even there—
your sheets; your own pillow's scent different.
As if daily someone repaints your room,
displaces something,
disturbs a cherished memento.

You see,
sometimes we *are* emptied.
We are emptied
Because
Life wants us to know

so

much

more

Light.

You Are a Precious Occurrence

Dear Young Seeker,

We are more capable and magnificent as sentient beings that many of us realize, and it is a fact that we can choose the emotions that best serves us to feel, no matter what is happening. Yes, even in the face of our own death. Perhaps *especially* in the face of our own death.

This could be one of the most significant letters I have written to you, in terms of the impact it can have on your life. Not only can you choose the emotion that you wish to feel at any moment, you can do so *ahead of time.*

Yes, you can do so before a moment arrives, given that you can very often anticipate a certain event or interaction. You may not always be able to choose the *thoughts* that come up for you when you sense that

69

you may be faced with certain circumstances or events, but you *can* choose, deliberately and intentionally, *the energy that you put into motion* after experiencing your thoughts.

In specific terms, you can intend for your emotion to be a source of healing, and never of hurting, an invitation for alteration, and never of altercation. This tells us who you are, and choose to be, as a person in the world.

Now I know that some people hold as their understanding that emotions are the inevitable result of certain thoughts. Here's the news, however. It is not an "absolute" that negative thinking must always produce negative emoting. If we make a decision ahead of time that even if we experience an urge to put negative energy into motion, we will change that decision and project our energy only in a positive way, we can generate real-world outcomes which are often more favorable than we might have imagined possible.

And so, we come to...

Inner Awareness #12
The experience of life that you most often produce is the result of the emotions that you most often project.

This is not something that anyone ever told me when I was young. As I've said, I heard a lot about thought as a force in generating our reality, but no one ever said, "It is the emotion that you choose, *following* a thought that you hold, which plays the biggest role in producing your next experience."

Nor did anyone ever share this with me: "You can choose all emotions ahead of time—not as a reaction to events, but as a creator of events."

That little piece of information, had it been given to me between ages 19 and 29, would have changed my life. Gone would have been 95% of the turmoil and disruption, to say nothing of what I mentioned in my third letter the pain I caused others.

Now wouldn't you like to avoid all of that? You can. But first, you must know why, and how, it is your emotions, rather than your thoughts, which are the most powerful elements of your life in creating your future.

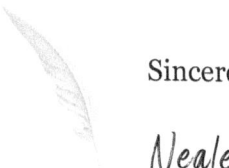

Sincerely,

Neale

I am a precious occurrence,
and I don't have long.
We are a precious occurrence.
And as long as we *think* we have,
we don't have long.
Too much time is being spent
running
from face to face
asking, "What is my name?"

If you don't yet know it,
or if you've forgotten,
then become still, go within
and answer it.

You are a Precious Occurrence:
Tell *Us* your name.

It's a Beautiful Time
To Be Alive

Dear Young Seeker,

There is a reason that your emotions can create your future. It is a powerful reason, and one that you may not have thoroughly explored before. The reason is that *your* emotions produce emotions in *others*.

Now that simple statement may seem like something which is obvious to you, but what *causes* that effect may not be quite as apparent. And until you know the cause of this effect, simply knowing about it may not be near enough to make your life better. So, let's look at that, shall we?

Your emotions produce emotions in others because, in the strictest sense, there *are* no "others." There is no separation between you and anyone else. And the closer you are emotionally to a person, the more your singularity (not to be confused with uniformity) becomes self-evident.

What you feel—and especially what you project by expressing emotions—others feel. This is so because, to put it figuratively, there is no one else in the room.

That principle is reducible to four words, offered here as...

Inner Awareness #13
We are all One.

Scientists are now affirming, having for years explored the basic elements of rocks brought back from the moon and objects which have fallen to Earth from outer space, that everything in the cosmos is made of the same stuff. It is simply the arrangement of this "stuff" that differs from one object and one being to another. But those differences do not produce divisions, only dissimilarities in appearance.

In short, we may *look* separate from each other, but we are merely varying expressions of the same fundamental energy and, like fingers on the same hand, are all part of one body, and thus, of each other.

Now if you are not careful, you could hear this as little more than esoteric meandering. But it is a surprisingly practical and powerfully useful piece of information.

When we realize that the energy we send out, through every emotion we project, is felt by others—particularly those in close proximity to us—we have reached clarity about one of the most significant and important aspects of daily life, because the events of our daily life are being *co-created*, not singularly produced by any of us alone

One way to create and produce a joyful life, therefore, is to choose to express and project to those others who are your co-creators, only those emotions which you would like to experience surrounding and enveloping yourself.

Now again, to reiterate what was said in a previous letter, this does not mean to "fake it," or to deny a negative emotion, but rather, to deliberately re-shape it, and then genuinely experience it. Used consistently and tenaciously in this way, this process can be a mighty means of transforming not only an important moment, but your whole life, by transforming the life of those whose life you touch. For they will very often create positive energy in your life, even as you create positive energy in theirs. Yet this is not the reason to do it. Those expressing pure love do not give to others, to get something back.

So, when life brings us positive energy back, it is not a matter of manipulation, but a matter of manifestation. And, in our manifestation process, we can deliberately choose positive emotions not only in any moment, but—as I've emphasized here—*ahead of time*.

More specifics about this in our next letter. It's information you don't want to miss.

Sincerely,

Neale

It's a beautiful time to be alive.
And the long walk home is peopled—
We are *everywhere*.
Yet the struggle to *surrender*
is where we often walk alone.
So the next time you fall,
look to either side where you lie
and take the hand
of your dear Brother or Sister
whose own clothes are muddied.
We can rise together,
even if we fall alone.
For it's a beautiful time to be alive,

even
on this
long
walk
home

The Sweet Unveiling

Dear Young Seeker,

I've made the point repeatedly now that it is not necessary to wait until an event occurs, or a circumstance develops, to choose the emotion you wish to express. You can choose your emotion well before any particular event or circumstance arises—even unexpected ones. And this can be especially empowering in the case of those which are unwelcome.

Now, let's explore that more fully.

While it is not true in every single case, many people often know ahead of time, or can make a pretty good, educated guess about what is likely to happen— or at least what is very possible—in the days or times ahead.

Given this ability, we can decide right now how we are going to react if our "inner prediction" should come true.

Let me give you an example of what I mean when I say we can choose our emotion ahead of time. Very few people walk into a funeral service howling with laughter or joyfully smiling ear-to-ear while greeting a decedent's grievers—even if, to ease the tension, we did just share a good laugh in the car with someone who drove with us to the memorial service.

Likewise, we would not attend a loved one's college graduation ceremony glum with sadness, or greet the celebrant with lugubrious tears, even if we did just hear a song sung at the ceremony which brought back sad memories for us.

We observe, then, that we have each already demonstrated the ability to quite deliberately choose emotions that—let's see, how to put this...that "match the moment." In doing so, we are deciding how we want the moment to be.

And yes, we can also do this when what might be expected in a specific moment may not be so patently obvious. We can even come up with exactly the opposite of what might be expected. When we do so, we can turn a potentially sad or worrisome moment into one of serenity and tranquility.

Again, this is not about submerging or sublimating what one naturally feels. It is about deciding what one *chooses* to feel, even if it seems unusual.

This would be a good place to repeat 34 words that appeared in my letter *What Is It That You Were Given?* "Even anger can be expressed lovingly. So too, frustration. And, as well, disappointment or disapproval. It turns out that any thought which one would define as negative can be expressed in a positive way."

There is a term used in legal cases, called "malice aforethought." What I am proposing here is "benevolence aforethought." This brings us to...

Inner Awareness #14

The person who decides ahead of time
to express and project benevolent emotions
creates a future filled with benevolence
for the self and others.

Many human beings yearn for more peace and less turmoil in their lives. They may not, however, have thought of, or even heard of using this approach as a means of creating it.

The approach again? Substitute positive emotion for thought as the tool most used in the process of manifestation.

Norman Vincent Peale wrote a book in 1952 which became world famous, titled *The Power of Positive Thinking*. I think it's time for a new book, titled *The Power of Positive Emotions*.

And now, I am moved to share with you in our next letter a secret about life which, once embraced as our reality, can make it natural for you to *always* feel like emoting positively, even in the face of loss.

Sincerely,

Neale

The sweet Unveiling is so becoming
there is perhaps nothing
more beautiful.

The *glide* that you once called
"walking".

Your fears
dropped as gently as lingerie.

As Who You Are,
naked child,
turns every purpose
Lightward—
toward what has always been

right
here
shining
as

You.

Lay Me Down in Love

Dear Young Seeker,

*M*any people on our planet experience life as a win/lose proposition.

If they are hoping to find and enter a wonderful relationship, they see themselves either winning or losing in that effort. If they want to create the perfect career or level of income, they see themselves either winning or losing in that endeavor. If they find themselves in an argument with an important other person, they see themselves either winning or losing in that exchange.

Even if all they want is a peaceful, happy life of positive experiences, they see themselves most often either winning or losing in that encounter. Much of humanity's entire experience of events and circumstances of everyday existence is very often viewed in this context.

This is not a small matter, because it can make it extraordinarily difficult to embrace and project positive emotions when we feel we are losing in what we see as life's ongoing battles. And we *see* life as a series of "battles" for a fascinating—if totally inaccurate—reason. In one word: insufficiency. Put into a simple sentence: We think there is "not enough."

There are not enough people who are truly open and unafraid to be loving, to go around, or we would easily be able to experience a wonderful relationship. There are not enough opportunities to express our particular talents, or we would easily be able to experience a fabulous career and our perfect income. There is not enough common sense being expressed by others, or we would easily be able to experience a life without arguments. And there is not enough just plain goodness in our daily life, or we would easily be able to experience days and nights which offer sufficient peace, comfort, and positive experiences for us to be happy.

But now, we come upon a question. What if we are wrong about that? What it there is more than enough of all the things that we think are lacking in life? What if we are simply not seeing it, or looking at it in that way? Could a change of mind about this produce a change of life?

Please let me share with you—before you get too much older and possibly become cynical or pessimistic—that there is no need to continually be frustrated as you seek to create a happy daily experience.

This will become your truth if and when you incorporate into your life...

Inner Awareness #15
There's enough.

If people around the world embraced this truth, the collective experience of life on this planet would soar to high heaven with positive outcomes and joyful moments.

Your life can soar just like that right now. That is why I am sharing this with you. My long life has shown me that there is enough of everything I very often thought there was not enough of. There's enough time, there's enough opportunity, there's enough love, there's enough security, there's enough money, there's enough food to go around for everyone.

There's no need for any person to go to bed hungry every night. There's no need for any person to be living without needed medicines. There's no need for any person to experience abject poverty. There's no need for any person to fall into loneliness or deep depression. There's enough of what all of us desire in our lives for all of us to experience everything in our lives. All we have to do is share.

One of the biggest hidden truths of my first 60 years on this planet is that all I have to do is give away whatever it is that I wish for more of in life, and much of what I desire will come to me. Ah, but that won't happen if I do it for this reason, because then I am giving nothing away, but only using a form of taking. I am serving myself, and my need to serve myself is nothing but an announcement of what I feel that I lack in sufficient amount. And what I feel is what I will experience.

If, on the other hand, I give what I wish to experience more of, not because I wish for more, but because when I am aware that I already have enough to give to others who do *not* have nearly enough (if any), I transform my experience from lack to sufficiency.

This has been, for me, a *huge* insight about life: My giving anything away creates the experience of sufficiency in me. This applies to material things (money I give to a homeless person, clothes I take to Goodwill, etc.) and that which is non-physical (offering to others my time, acceptance, understanding, friendship, a willing ear, forgiveness...and, of course, love).

Embracing this insight and employing it in your life as a truly loving way to be, can move you forward massively in the process of your evolution.

Sincerely,

Neale

Lay me down in Love.
Anoint my thoughts in such a way
that Heaven's supply of Lovebreath
will almost run out today.

Bless my knees with Love.
Ready them for all those times ahead.
In me you have found a Love-soldier,
and one more loyal to This Cause than any.

As many ways as there are to Love,
let me know them then.
Let's decide, God,
that I am *already*

A
Graduate.

Speak in a Soul Language

Dear Young Seeker,

It's perhaps a good time now to turn to the broader subject of morals in this discussion. I'm talking about basic human moral values.

Does our species consider it to be a reflection of our highest collective morals to allow many people to go to bed hungry every night? Is it a reflection of our highest moral values to knowingly allow any person to live without desperately needed medicines, because there's not enough profit in it for those medicines to be supplied?

There are many other questions such as this that could be asked, because our human society has made more than a few wrong turns as we seek to advance in our evolution. One of those other questions could be: Is it a reflection of the highest moral value to condemn?

Here is my answer: Condemnation—of self or others—does neither any good. The answer is not to condemn ourselves for any of the wrong turns we have made, collectively or individually, but to determinedly set a new course when we see we are making, or have made, a major mistake.

So, if you have made a wrong turn in your life (...and who hasn't...), do not be so hard on yourself (or others) that you can't forgive. In fact, forego forgiveness altogether. Seek, instead, to understand why certain behaviors arose.

Then, empowered by that understanding, offer compassion and healing love to others, and yes, to yourself if you were one making the wrong turn. This leads us to...

Inner Awareness #16
*Understanding replaces forgiveness
in the mind of the master.*

Think of the difference it would make in the life of another who may have offended or injured you in some way, if you said to them: "I understand how this could have happened. I don't agree with it. I don't approve of it. But I can understand it, because I have said or done some of the same kinds of things in my life. And we can move past this. I hope you will agree to do so with me."

That kind of approach—speaking from your highest self with someone who has upset you—could change your relationship with that person, *and* with *yourself,* in ways that are more wonderfully beneficial than you might be able to imagine.

Offering *forgiveness* to another says to that person that you feel they have done something wrong, but you are going to grant them a pardon. Offering *understanding,* on the other hand, does not require the other person to feel ashamed or guilty. It simply allows them to look at their behavior and see if they can understand not only their own feelings, but why *you* feel the way *you* do.

So, offer compassionate understanding in *place* of forgiveness, and watch the energetic vibration of your life change in ways that produce wonderfully positive interactions—with yourself and others.

Sincerely,

Neale

Speak in a Soul Language
so that Everyone can
hear.
Restore This Story of Humanity
with a
presence so precious,
no words could give it definition.

Practice loving so deeply
that the word for tears
becomes
"ocean"
and
the School of Compassion
is this
World's Greatest Institution.

Let no one walk alone
on this journey that is
Ours
to share:

Speak in a Soul Language,
so that Everyone can hear.

Be Received

Dear Young Seeker,

I want to share with you now another life tool that could also change forever, in a wonderfully positive way, how you react to everybody and everything you disagree with.

Sometime shortly after my 50th year on this planet I came to the realization that there are very few things that are "right" or "wrong" in and of themselves. A thing is only right and wrong because I say it is. "Rightness" or "wrongness" is not an intrinsic condition; it is a subjective judgment arising from a personal value system.

Put another way, what I might think is absolutely right in one situation, I might think is positively wrong in another. And vice versa. The disagreements and condemnation we have seen (and continue to see every day) between people and nations bear testimony to that.

A good example of this is the death penalty. Is it wrong to kill someone intentionally because they killed someone intentionally? Or is it right to kill someone intentionally because they did the same thing?

Well, one might say, it all depends on what it is we are trying to do. Are we trying to reduce the number of instances in our society in which individuals kill other individuals intentionally, or are we seeking to make sure that a person who has done so never does so again, and pays for what they have done in equal measure?

If we're trying to bring an end to, or reduce the number of, individuals killing other individuals intentionally, it has not worked. Statistics have made that very clear.

The eminent 20th century scientist Albert Einstein offered humanity this observation: "You will not solve any problem using the same energy which created it."

And we have seen that he was right. We have not been able to bring an end to anger with anger, bring an end to violence with violence, bring an end to killing with killing, and so on.

The solution to this dilemma is for all of us to create a way to disagree agreeably. And you can find that path by embracing (as radical as it may sound, at first) a new understanding about right and wrong. I call this...

Inner Awareness #17

There's no such thing as absolute right and wrong. There is only what works, and what does not work, given what it is you are trying to do.

If you decide that "right" and "wrong" are not absolutes, but only stances you take that reflect your present value system (which, itself, may change through the years), you will most likely create a life with far fewer intense arguments, far fewer inflicted hurts, far fewer lost friends, far fewer ended relationships, and far fewer searing and tearful regrets in your own final years.

This does not mean never allow yourself to experience a disagreement, but it does mean that striving to find a way to *disagree agreeably* will always serve you in the short term and could pay humongous dividends in the long term.

This new way of being could involve changing some old patterns in the way you've often responded to others.

Don't feel you have to do this overnight. Give yourself time to make any adjustment, if one is even needed, in your usual initial reaction to differences of opinion.

Simply look to see if the way you are disagreeing works or does not work, based on what it is you are wishing to do—such as keep a relationship going in a healthy and joyful way, maintain a meaningful friendship, hold onto a job, create harmonious interactions with neighbors or strangers, or simply experience ongoing peace and serenity in your day-to-day life.

Sincerely,

Neale

Move slowly from these old skins.
Your belly is raw, your back is tender—
you are rudimentary now.

Move softly from these old skins.
Let the full bodyweight
of all your innocence
down.

Be received.
Be received by the broad earth of your worthiness.
Cast off everything
everyone else has known for you.

Move gratefully from these old skins.

And this time, if you toughen,
decide

for whom?

Go Outside and Play

Dear Young Seeker,

I'm glad you're still here with me. Thank you for reading as far as you have and having the intellectual curiosity and emotional determination to do so. As I said in my first letter, we need more young people like you if our species is going to create a new and better tomorrow.

With that in mind, I would like to now explore what I have come to know as the Be-Do-Have Paradigm. Again, this is something that no one ever explained to me when I was in my teens, or my 20s. And that is sad, because it's one of the most important aspects of human existence that I've ever come to understand, and it would have changed so many, many unwelcome moments in my life.

I'd like to give you some examples of what I thought, because of what my culture taught me, when I was moving through those early years.

I thought that...

...when I finally *have* what I call enough time, I can *do* the thing called pay attention to what really matters in my life, and I can *be* the thing called "peaceful and content."

...when I finally *have* what I call a good job, I can *do* the thing called perform well, and I can then *be* the thing called "happy at work."

...when I finally *have* what I call a good relationship, I can *do* the thing called get married, and I can then *be* the thing called "no-longer-lonely in my soul."

I deliberately italicized the same words in all of those sentences, because there seemed to me to be what television script writers would call this through-line of Have-Do-Be in the story called Life: If I *have* what I need to have, I can *do* what I need to do, and then I can *be* what I wish to be.

Only after ongoing and repeated experiences did I come to realize that there is a formula for life, alright, and it does involve having, doing, and being---- but that I had it all backward.

That's right. Totally backward. Completely reversed. The most powerful life formula is Be-Do-Have.

How it works is to *start out* "being" what you wish to be. In other words, come *from* that place, rather than try to get *to* that place. Then, do what any person, if they are being what they wish to be, would most naturally do. You will then experience having what you'd hoped to have in life.

Now I know that deserves an illustration, to see how it could actually work. So here goes.

If I choose *ahead of time* to *be* the thing called "peaceful and content," I will quite naturally *do* the thing called pay attention to what really matters in life, and then I will find that I *have* what is called "enough time." This is because our ability to use time wisely expands when we are peaceful and content.

If I choose *ahead of time* to *be* "happy at work" because I experience that being employed is better than being unemployed, I will quite naturally *do* the thing called perform well, and then I will find that I *have* what is called a good job. This is because employers are not drawn to keep people employed who are unhappy with their job, but value people who are not.

If I choose *ahead of time* to *be* "no-longer-lonely in my soul," I can *do* the thing called get married, then I will find that I *have* what is called a good relationship. This is because potential life partners are not drawn to people who are lonely, but people who are not.

Now, another fair question: How can a person *be* something, if they don't *have* what they need to *have*, to *do* what they need to *do*, to *be* what they wish to *be?*

The answer is that "being" is an *act of will*. It is an action, not a reaction. It is a decision, not a revision. We are not *revising* our state of inner-being because of events that have occurred, we are *devising* our state of inner-being before events occur, out of our realization that what we do and have in life arises *from* how we are being in the world, rather than taking us *to* how we are being.

I notice that our species has been called human beings, not human doings, and not human havings. Therefore, decide how you choose to be in your life, no matter what you are doing or having, and if you choose to be positive, sensitive to others, compassionate, understanding, and loving, watch how it can dramatically improve what you wind up having.

Let me put this into one sentence, which I have called...

Inner Awareness #18

*The Be-Do-Have paradigm
can produce wonderful outcomes,
allowing you to enjoy your life
as never before.*

Sincerely,

Neale

"Go outside and play!"
said God.
"I have given you Universes as fields to run free in!
And here—take this and wrap yourself in it—
it's called *LOVE,*
and it will always, *always* keep you warm.

And the stars! Oh, the sun and the moon and the
stars!
Look upon these often, for they will remind you
of your own light!
And eyes . . . oh, gaze into *every* Lover's eyes.
Gaze into every Other's eyes—
for they have given you *their* Universes
as fields to run free in.
There.
I have given you everything you need.

Now go, go, *go outside* and PLAY!"

Make Amends with How Things Are

Dear Young Seeker,

As we draw near the end of my series of letters, I hope that you feel you've benefitted by having called forth from within you, and thus remembered, much of what you already knew intuitively to be true. And if you disagreed with one or two (or more) of the statements found here, I'm totally okay with that.

This does not mean that I am not a man of conviction, but it does mean that I do not mentally convict those who do not convinced. I came to an awareness long ago that life becomes more challenging, and often more downright disappointing, when I embrace a state of mind in which I turn something I *desire* into something I *require* to be content with my experience.

This wasn't the case with me in the first three decades of my adult life. I *did* require particular and specific responses, reactions, and results in my life. I placed requirements on myself and, I'm sorry to say on others.

One unforeseen outcome of this is that even when I got what I wanted, I often felt victimized by what it took for that to happen. This allowed me to be both the hero and the victim of my own story, simultaneously.

Even worse, there are others who have felt victimized by me, and that is something that, for me, no number of my apologies can undo. So, I have come to a place in my life where there continues to be that which I desire, but very little of that which I require.

Now I know from past public interactions and discussions of this with large audiences that there are those who will say, "You require air to breathe, food to eat, clothing to wear, and shelter, don't you?"

It's true, of course. But I'm sure you're clear that we're not talking about requirements for physical survival here. We are talking about what can cause us to be at peace, to be serene and content. We are exploring what can allow us to feel happy with our life, assuming we are not in this moment being physically attacked or verbally assaulted.

There is much going on in our world that is robbing people of their peace, their serenity, their happiness, and even their safety...and I don't want you to think that I am oblivious to that or suggesting that the world should ignore it. My commentary here is offered in a context that I hope with all my heart that you are presently experiencing. That is, a life where you are not now being assaulted or assailed.

That said, I'll share with you...

Inner Awareness #19

Do not change what you desire
into something you require.

This does not mean that you should have no goals in life, but I believe (and I have experienced) that we are most well served when we have few or no "musts" regarding results generated by our efforts, few or no absolutes in terms of other people's behavior, and few or no prerequisites in terms of the accoutrements of life.

Sincerely,

Neale

Believe me, you don't have to know.
Not so much that you render yourself helpless.
Helpless in the face of what life brings next.
So make peace with knowing very little.
About Love.
About Others.
About how Life *should* be.
Make amends with how things Are.
Not knowing a thing,
walk with gentle knees,
ready to drop to them
at any moment
that Life dictates it.
Keep an empty hand
so that it may be brought to your heart
when a Grief arrives.
Make up a bed
that you can fall into
as your own comforting arms.

We come to find that Life is mostly Quiet.
It asks us to live by our Knowing,
while surrendering that very same thing.
It vibrates easily around Us,
candid, and benevolent.

You see, it's only when
we are solid in a knowing again
that Life seems to have to shout –
rises, Lovingly, from Its whisper.

One Step at a Time

Dear Young Seeker,

We have only two letters left, and in this second-to-last dispatch, I want to share a very brief – and yet what I have found to be a very powerful – piece of advice that my father offered to me frequently.

When I was a young person, I worried very often about things that could happen. I could fail the course. I could not get the job. I could lose a friend. I could hurt myself playing football. I could not win the heart of the lady I loved. I could...I could...I could...

This turned into a bunch of "what if" questions. What if I do *not* get the job? What if I *am* hurt on the playing field? What if I *do* lose my best friend? And these are all personal, individual issues. Today, with the world in the condition it's in, we could be in for some very difficult times collectively. We are facing major human-created challenges politically, economically, environmentally, and spiritually—to say nothing about items completely out of our control (earthquakes, tornadoes, or even stray meteors striking Earth).

How, then, to find even a modicum of happiness in our life, not to mention bringing happiness to the lives of others?

I have concluded that my father's oft-articulated advice has served me well since I began taking it to heart after worrying through my 20s, 30s, and 40s. His advice? "Son, cross that bridge when you come to it."

Since I began doing that, my day-to-day mood has elevated significantly. And I've also noticed something. Most of the things I worried about never actually happened. I won't say none, but maybe two out of ten. And I've found that "bad stuff" at a level of 20% in my life is not worth giving up my inner joy or my outer happiness.

This goes back to what we explored in a previous letter, which is that life almost always says yes to what we think about the most.

Please allow me to now amplify that insight with...

Inner Awareness #20

Because what you anticipate, you often propagate, it works best to cross each bridge when you come to it.

Sincerely,

Neale

And the mind said, "How will I handle all of it?"

Then, before the mind could answer,
something akin to a whisper
—a presence with a Lover's touch—
stirred within me,
saying:

"One step at a time."

A great way opened up just then,

and through the air, each foot rose and fell;
each sole met and kissed
the stones

One Step at a Time

the Now, a lover,

Her

body

draped

just

so

What Could Be Your Best Decision Ever

Dear Young Seeker,

*I*n my final letter, I'm going to share what I consider to be the single most amazing life secret I've ever encountered.

Yes, I've saved the best for last. As wonderfully useful and truly beneficial as I believe each other Awareness to be, I consider my closing offering to be the most sensational, in terms of the joyful and bountiful results it can produce.

Let's get to it, then, and eliminate any suspense. To conclude our interactions in this book, here is...

Inner Awareness #21

The most powerful way to experience what you wish to experience in your life is not to be a seeker, but to be the source.

For the first three decades of my adult life, I felt that the one of the most spiritually beneficial things I could do was to be what is called "a seeker." I felt humble and proud to experience myself in this way, and I saw it as the shortest and fastest path to what has been termed "enlightenment" and "mastery in living."

Then I discovered that *seeking* what I hoped to experience in life was not the most effective way to create what I wished for. I found that being the *source* in the life of *others* of what I wanted in *my* life was the path I was looking for.

This works for two reasons. The first reason is explored in Inner Awareness #14: We Are All One. This means that what I do for you, I do for me because in reality there is only one of us.

The second reason is that, even if a person does not embrace the notion that we are all one, the energetics of life work in such a way that what flows through you sticks to you. As I mentioned earlier, the energy that you project outward acts as a magnet which draws the same energy to you.

This is just a longer way of articulating a statement you may have heard before: "What goes around, comes around."

Here's another statement you may have heard

before: "Do unto others as you would have it done unto you." Now that was a wonderful piece of advice.

So, if you want more abundance in your life, cause another to have more in theirs. Never pass a homeless person without dropping whatever you can spare in the basket next to their sign which says: "Anything helps."

If you want more positivity and more happiness in your life, cause another to have more in theirs. A simple smile shared with a stranger in the post office, or a complimentary comment about their efficiency shared with a checkout person at the grocery store, can change a person's day.

This list could go on.

When I first heard about this idea, I decided, as an experiment, to no longer be a seeker, but to always be a source. I looked closely to see what I truly wished I had more of in my life, then I looked for people who had even less of it than I had, and I became a source of it for them.

It worked.

I strongly encourage you to make the same choice. It could be your best decision ever. You may find that it's like magic, because you have become a "sorcerer," creating what you've wanted more of in your life by showing yourself that you actually already have it. Enough, in fact, to give some away.

This can be a remarkable illumination. In fact, it can be one of the most powerful realizations of your life. It certainly was for me, and it is the very reason that I've written you the letters you've read here.

I've stopped wishing for greater understanding in my life and only wish now to offer more understanding to others. I've stopped wishing for more awareness in my life and only wish now to offer more awareness to others. I've stopped wishing for more goodness in my life and only wish now to offer more goodness to others. I've stopped wishing for more love in my life and only wish now to offer more love to others.

I'll close this collection of letters to you with this invitation: Try the approach explored above. Commit to offering more understanding, more awareness, more goodness, and more love to everyone whose life you touch, and see what happens. End your time as a seeker and begin your time as a source. I'm betting that you will become resource *full*.

Sincerely,

Neale

In place of a poem…

I'd like to offer here, as a closing note, this passage from *Conversations with God-Book One*/Chapter 3…

You are goodness and mercy and compassion and understanding.

You are peace and joy and light.

You are forgiveness and patience, strength and courage, a helper in time of need, a comforter in time of sorrow, a healer in time of injury, a teacher in times of confusion.

You are the deepest wisdom and the highest truth; the greatest peace and the grandest love.

You are these things. And in moments of your life you have known yourself as these things. Choose now to know yourself as these things always.

Afterword

Thank you for reading these 21 letters. I have one favor to ask. If you feel that anything you found here has value, please pass that value on to others.

Nobody has to tell us that life on our planet is not what we had hoped it would be. All we have to do is take a look at what's happening every day around the world—and in some cases, in our own lives.

There are very few among us who have not found ourselves shaking our head in discouraged dismay at the latest social media post or online news bulletin or newspaper headline. And sometimes—too many times, perhaps—at the challenges confronted in our home.

This leads to a compelling question: Is it possible— just *possible*—that there's something we don't fully remember about ourselves, about life, and about God, the remembering of which would change everything?

To me the answer is obviously yes. And saying "yes" to that question is what would help us to see that this is a time to be the source of that which we wish to see more of in our lives, and in our world.

I begin to think now of other questions that I believe it would be very helpful for people everywhere to ask.

What if the most wonderful ideas you ever had about life were true?

What if the most wonderful ideas you ever had about yourself were true?

What if the most wonderful ideas you ever had about God were true?

What if the most wonderful ideas you ever had about what happens after you die were true?

What would then be true for you?

Do you think there would be any difference between how you might *then* experience life and how you *now* experience life?

Your answers to these questions are now setting the course and direction of your experience on Earth. Not to be overly dramatic about it, but it's true. They are determining the path you will take.

It is *because* this is true that I thank you for reading these letters and passing them on.

Let this be not just *my* afterword, but *your* afterword, too.

Poetry Index

Following is a list of the Em Claire poems found in this book, with a notation on when they were written.

Letter #18: Go Outside and Play, ©2007
Letter #19: Life Is Mostly Quiet ©2006
Letter #20: One Step at a Time, ©2010

Note: The poem *When Did You Stop Singing?* was inspired by an excerpt in a book by Gabrielle Roth, *Maps to Ecstasy (New World Library, Novato, CA. 1998)*. Permission was granted by Gabrielle Roth to include this four-line stanza in the Em Claire poem.

Author Bios

Neale Donald Walsch is the author of multiple books, including six New York Times bestsellers. Titles in his *Conversations with God* series have been translated into 37 languages. Among his other works: *Friendship with God, Communion with God, What God Wants, Tomorrow's God, Home With God (in a Life That Never Ends), GodTalk,* and *The God Solution.* He has traveled the globe offering lectures and programs helping people to integrate the spiritual principles of *Conversations with God* into their daily lives.

His website: www.nealedonaldwalsch.com.

Em Claire was born and raised in the Northwest of the United States. Her award-winning first book of poetry, *Silent Sacred Holy Deepening Heart,* was followed by a second compilation titled, *Home Remembers Me,* both of which became studio recording collections read by the author. She is a writer of poetry and prose, an artist, and musician. She calls Ashland, Oregon her home, where she met her husband, Neale Donald Walsch.

Other works by Em Claire may be found at her website: emclairepoet.love.